THE BOOK OF

SOL

R. D. SOLOMON JR.

THE BOOK OF SOL

Copyright © 2016 Rowdy Solomon Jr.

All rights reserved. No part of this book may be reproduced or transmitted in any form or by any means, electronic or mechanical, including photocopying, recording, or by any information storage and retrieval system, without permission in writing from the publisher. All questions and/or request are to be submitted to: 134 Andrew Drive, Reidsville NC, 27320.

To the best of said publisher knowledge, this is an original manuscript and is the sole property of author **ROWDY SOLOMON Jr.**

Printed in the United States of America

ISBN-13:978-0692744659
ISBN-10:0692744657

Printed by Createspace 2016

Published by BlaqRayn Publishing Plus 2016

Introduction

The Book Of Sol is poetry originated from the very depths of Rowdy D. Solomon Jr. deriving from his early works in 2010 all the way up to this present day.

Many of the works have been shuffled around and placed carefully throughout the book for versatility and to simply keep you interested.

Many of the literary works are indeed personal and some provide a shield over the actual events that took place so you would never know what really happened to motivate him to write it.

The Book of SOL

Every page is full of wonder, suspense and soul.

THE BOOK OF

SOL

R. D. SOLOMON JR.

The Book of SOL

I AM POETRY

My mind is an incubator. It hatches embryos divinely planted into it over a period of time. These embryos are ideas, topics, and experiences that were fed, nurtured and given life through my thoughts. These thoughts become words, carefully constructed and crafted with each syllable having a heartbeat of its own. I speak these words, and they grow arms and legs to position themselves in a precise formation on the piece of paper I stare at with each breath I take forming a new word... forming a new life... a new beginning.... My eyes project these words across horizons too far

The Book of SOL

for the "human eye" to take notice of. Genres and styles flow through my veins and filter through my heart for approval and editing. For these reasons I have to keep an open mind... an open heart.... Moods for these compositions are set and can be changed instantly by a simple word or phrase, so I must watch what I think, say, and write. These words lives could be someone's death if I use them the wrong way. This gift... this power.... is not one taken lightly. It must be mastered and re-mastered with every "new beginning"...

I's" are dotted with my saliva. "t's" are cross my heart and I hope to die with a sense of

The Book of SOL

perfection in mind being perfectly imperfect. With each step I take, as my foot hits the ground on an evening stroll, it syncs with the exhale of my breath for the forming of a new word or phrase. My organs are a factory containing conveyor belts where countless messages are formed. I ingest these messages through my nostrils, eyes, and ears. They are moved through my digestive tract and are regurgitated onto a page and then later ingested by someone else through their eyes or ears. I must be careful to watch my intake, for I need to be healthy and a living example for those around me. I walk around and people look at me and my contents They look at me and take me out of context. They

The Book of SOL

often read me with the adverse perception for what I really am intended to show. However, there are a few with the same like spirit who actually can read between my lines that life has given me and see me for who I really am. However, my goal and my true purpose is to give you something to think about... Since I am full, I cannot leave others hungry...

Every texture my hand touch becomes an easel on which words are pasted, painting a picture of a poem I perceive. I have diction at my fingertips, and style on my side. It is as if I am King Midas. The only difference is everything I touch turns to poetry.

The Book of SOL

Furthermore, I have not just touched things physically. I touch lives. I touch spirits. I touch situations. Ways out have been given my hand, endowed with the divine power from above. I am a vessel and my hands are the release valve from the mere stroke of my pen. I can grab hold of anything and open it wide and write what is inside. My hands are analytical; to my eyes there is never a surprise. My insides are where ideas are supplied and my mind are where they reside. My feet are my vehicle for my eyes and ears to look and see around. My God is the one who created me to make this crooked mind of mine divine. I am what I write. I write what I am. I live it daily and sleep on it

The Book of SOL

nightly. This is my life, which is why I can bring life to it. I can even revive other dead ones when I see them laying on their sides motionless and hopeless. I simply am the pen I stroke. I am the words I say. I am the periods I put at the end of a line... and until the end of my line and even after... I will always say. I AM POETRY!!!

The Book of SOL

I CALL HER BEAUTY

Some call her sexy

Some call her a dime

Others see her for what is on the outside

But I see her true "color" and

I can read between the "lines"

Her texture is beyond measure

She is velvet to the touch

And plush to the squeeze

Her eyes make me cry

Her voice tingles my soul

And washes it clean

Her siblings call her blessed

Her mother calls her baby

My heart calls her mine

The Book of SOL

But from what I see on the inside

I call her beauty...

Her life is in her smile

She has endured more than the eye

And mind could perceive

Her hands have healing power

She has more than once

Made me whole again

Her loyalty makes her royalty

Even my anointing has to bow

Before her presence when she is presented

Past me in the present

Some don't call her anything because of

Awe

Some call her princess

The Book of SOL

Others call her enchanting

I call her beauty...

Her shine hits me... It's strikingly

Resembling to the sun itself

Because I heat up when I see her

Sometimes I feel like I don't even

Deserve her light of day

Because of things I did to her

Some nights

Yet, she is still my lantern

To guide me through dark days

She is transparent to me

I see the scars beneath the scars

She hides nothing

It has come to the point to when I see her,

The Book of SOL

I see me "photo-synthesis"

Some call her flower

Some call her strong

Others call her sassy

I call her beauty

The Book of SOL

VIBIN

Sipping on a glass of red wine

While my ears are blessed

From the sounds of upbeat jazz

Reminiscing over long days

And short nights as I look around

And see what I've accomplished

Long way to go still

But I am proud

As my lady lays on my chest

I have to thank her in silence

She's resting her brain and body

She has worked just as hard as I

I look up towards heaven

The Book of SOL

And thank God for giving me

The strength and mindset

To continue to push

Though so many things

And people have tried to

Pull me down

You don't always have to

Turn up to celebrate

Tonight...

We're just vibin

The Book of SOL

YOUR TENDER TOUCH

My darling angel

Oh, how I long for the

Gentleness of your soft-textured

Grip encamping different extremities of me

I love the way it gives my body

Instruction to rest and be tranquil

Oh, how I awe for the warmness of your

Fingers to tickle my emotions

And surgically remove my physical pains

It feels like each carpal

Creates a tunnel to different parts of me

To clear any negativity

And help me lighten my loads

The Book of SOL

Each appendage is appointed

A designated area so none

Of me is ignored

You know all of the right

Places to touch and magnify

I love how you apprehend me

And make me your own

Not to control me...

But to connect with me

It's a mystery of how I tremble at your

Slightest interaction with me

I instantly slip into a joy-filled

Coma where my world becomes a

Land of no more

No more stress No more

drama no more arguments

The Book of SOL

No more low self- esteem no

More doubts or demonic powers

Coming against me no more

Worries....

Just me...

And your tender touch.

The Book of SOL

PURE ROMANCE

The air was on full blast

As we cuddled under the warm sheets

Bodies closer than

A baby in a mother's womb

She felt my heartbeat on her back

Harder than I wanted to beat it up

Her hands grazed my arms

Too and fro

Aroused were we in more ways than one.

She turned over and her eyes arrested me

With ecstasy and passion

Fire was transparent as we began to kiss

She explored every inch of me with her

The Book of SOL

tongue

And I.... Her

It was time to create timeless moments

It was time...

For pure romance...

Damn...

I'm still thinking about it

The Book of SOL

OUR GOOD NIGHT

Soft Jazz bands played on the radio

While I played with strings of her hair

The tunes matched our voices so good that

Our conversation should have been the

lyrics laid to it

Her leg overlapped mine and my other leg

Overlapped hers, intertwining them like

braids

Her breath kept hitting my neck just right

To keep me aroused and attentive

Her hands were healing to my pain

As she rubbed me to and fro

The vibration from my voice

Tickled her ears and makes her laugh

The Book of SOL

My reward was her smile

I felt complete with our bodies touching

Pulling us together is love...

A tangible but not seen magnetic attraction

I would not have it any other way

Her lips touched mine and I tasted the

Strawberry lip gloss she was wearing

It made me bite her lip gently and

Suck on her bottom lip for a while

Before she turned over and asked me to

Hold her tight

The music ended, and the last sounding note

by the

Saxophone was so on point that it also made

us

The Book of SOL

Drift off to sleep, ending....

Our good night.

The Book of SOL

FROM THE BOTTOM OF MY GLASS

Intoxication is by the only means I do so

I honestly cannot tolerate you sober

Alcohol awakens me from your horror

You are the complete opposite of what I dream of

I guess that makes you my nightmare that lays

Next to me every night...

Yet with each sip you look better and better

I need not worry about emotions with the numb feeling

And slurred speech I possess in this state of being

The Book of SOL

I stagger around and put on a crooked smile

To symbolize my tornado inside me I'm

hiding

I know it sounds selfish... I know...

It sounds worse than you make it seem

In actuality this fallacy of analogies

Is for you I don't want to hurt you

I don't want to break your heart

(But I do want to leave you) (You won't

give me a reason to)

Take my passion full of Patron

Immerse yourself in me while I talk through

Jack Daniels

Fill my sex meter full of Tequila

Yes... there you have it because that's

The only way you'll have it

The Book of SOL

Apparently some part of me has to truly

love you

In order for me to do bad to do good

Until I figure it out.... Just know.... I love

you... from the bottom of my glass.

The Book of SOL

STRANGERS

I've broken my back

For those I knew

Stabbed in the back by the same

I've given my last to

Those I know

Only to get stepped on and watch

Them grow

I have expressed love to relatives

And significant others

Only to be violated by them both

My girl kissed a guy I called my brother

And they say ...

Keep your friends close and your enemies

closer

The Book of SOL

With friends like I have, you do not need

enemies ...

I gave a flower to a random girl

It brightened her world

And the world around her

When she blushed and

Smiled with a thank you

I Helped a man up from a fall

He gave me 10 dollars

I did not know him at all

I told an old lady she looks nice today

She shed a tear because it brightened her day

I threw a little kid football

Back that fell into the street

He smiled with glee

The Book of SOL

After receiving the catch ...

I walk around now ...

In a world full of people

Most of which I do not know

But seem to be more connected to

Than the ones I do

Mama said do not talk to

Them but honestly

I think I like strangers.

The Book of SOL

ROSES

As I went for an evening stroll,

After the workload,

My eyes got bold,

When I saw this rose,

So many stories to it,

That are left untold,

So I decided to write about it

Using poetry and prose.

You see it had just rained,

And the blossoms were glistening,

And growing by the second,

Like enemies against me,

But it held a great message

The I glared even closer,

The Book of SOL

Cold on the outside,

But in warm it as a toaster,

So I thought of myself,

And then studied my anatomy,

To see this flower how,

In comparison matches me.

The only thing I could think of

To give me a start,

Was the door I just opened,

In my heart created clean.

Through the texture and detail.

To characteristics

It was so plain to me now,

I cannot believe I had missed it,

I opened my heart's door,

Just like this rose,

The Book of SOL

To see the beauty within

That evidently holds,

Serenades or melodies,

Even the words of Shakespeare,

Cannot compete with the beauty,

Of the picture it paints here.

Vibrant in color,

A great way to escape,

The pains in your life,

When they become too great.

Just say the rappers lyrics,

To receive awards and merits,

Hearts and roses open to us,

To be loved and cherished,

From the glistening majesty,

To a simple compliment,

The Book of SOL

The roses are bolded,

And the heart past dominant,

It's prominent ...

It gained its love now,

There is in stopping it,

But be careful how you treat them,

You cannot keep dropping it,

BOTH are gentle in nature,

So do not keep knocking it,

Against evil things, now the

Purpose for it is opposite.

There are plenty to go around,

The pushing and shoving,

If you plan on keeping mine,

Place no one above me,

Except the one who keeps us all

The Book of SOL

Because soon He will judge me,

But my heart is like a rose,

Always open, always loving ...

The Book of SOL

A DISTANT LAND

Away is where I wish to be

A place where bothers do not exist

Only peace and tranquility encamp me

In the fields of flowers

As the wind tickles my ears

Away ... where I can reside for a lifetime

And never grow old

Smiles are my constant facial expressions

And the tingly feeling down my spine never fades

I can always be me and I am

Always welcome to hide and seek

To be lost and found

The Book of SOL

To love and be loved

The birds will sing melodies for me

To match words to

The waters run clear and crisp

The smell of the air arouses me

Yes, away ... where my resting place is

anywhere

And I can be like a baby treated

Pampered to my every heart's desire

And I can feel born again

I have dreamed and daydreamed

Of this place often

Often and after losing the battle of doubt

My victory is

I do not have to wish or dream anymore

After years of searching

The Book of SOL

I found this place

in you

The Book of SOL

ANALYSIS OF YOUR ANATOMY

I started to wonder about the spots and

wrinkles over time

I have attained

Where did they come from? How Were

They formed?

I quickly formed the theory every wrinkle,

every ...

Scar or discoloration has a story to tell

Even if I myself with it being on this body I

have borrowed

Did not know its origin

I continued to explore my body and saw que

The Book of SOL

There were many stories on within it to be

told

I found that It is very unique in structure

The strong build from the sole of my feet to

the crown of my head

Some parts are larger than others but ...

They all coincide to connect and

complement one another

My chest sits on top of my abs like a crown

Showing my royalty

My legs support this beastly torso and neck

and shoulders

My arms spread like the wings of an angel

and wrap

Around others for their comfort

The Book of SOL

My fingers connect me to others putting the tingle down spines

And saying hello to places seen and unseen

Yes, this body does many things but it would be nothing without

The mind my skull protects

I challenge you ...

Take a little while to stare at yourself naked

See how amazing you really are

Get comfortable with yourself, so you can be more

Comfortable around others on a daily basis

Gain some confidence in who you are why don't you ...

Take a look. Take an

Analysis of your anatomy ....

The Book of SOL

CANDY

Caramel kisses with chocolate saliva

Hershey's kisses nipples atop

Double D Reese's cups

I get all the more the jolly

When you ride me like a rancher

Thrusting my snickers in between

Your twix-complexion legs

Sweating nerds as you rope your arms around me

Climaxing... hotter than a fireball

The Book of SOL

Dripping coconut all over your body

From my milky way

While you ooze flavors

From your fruit gushers

Mmmmmm....

I love candy

The Book of SOL

FLOW

Sitting by the river

Watching waters travel

So carefree and serene

In their motions and gestures

My eyes wandered to the

Scenery of rocks and debris

Along the edges and

In the river bank

Eroding and broken down

The Book of SOL

Were they from the constant

Nagging of the water

At its contents

Nothing stopped the water

Nothing stopped its direction

Its purpose... its determination

Its unremitting in conquering

The obstacles that troubled it

Whether it had to go around it

Under it, over it or just

Deal with over time

The Book of SOL

To get through it

The water ceased not

In its progress

Only to reciprocate and go

Again eventually

Much like the love so

Many of us are searching for...

Let it flow...

From one heart to another

Let it flow...

In your actions and through

The Book of SOL

The troubles of the world

Let it flow

Freely and not forced or

Just going through the motions

You want love?

Let it flow...

The Book of SOL

A FOOL'S CAMOUFLAGE

Trickery... the new reality

For some anyway

For others will find any way

To push lies to the limit

Pulling wool over your eyes

Not realizing... You have real eyes

To see real lies

The truth concealed behind smiles

And grins of wolves wearing cotton dresses

The Book of SOL

And polo shirts

Tones and eloquence emitting, covering

The stench of selfishness and ambition

Lingering from those spades called hearts

They really know how to play their cards

Wives and husbands

Causing trouble and

Boyfriends, fiances

Still searching for Beyoncé

Girlfriends and mistresses

On dating websites and

The Book of SOL

Having sexual relations with so

Called friends and people they can't stand

So they decide to lay with them

Am I telling the truth yet?

Bold enough to try to hide the truth in your face

To piss on you and tell you it's raining

To take from you and talk about what they have given

Please....

I'd rather dig my own hole before falling in someone else's

The Book of SOL

I speak for all loyal ones saying

I'm not oblivious, I just don't care anymore

I actually find it funny because

You aren't fooling anyone

You're just in a fool's camouflage.

The Book of SOL

ONE ON ONE

The night sky falls while I rise

The occasion of a spur of the moment

I feel like floating to wherever

The night takes me

Soothing sounds from my radio

Elevate the mood all the more

I have already soaked my worn

Body in the tub and rubbed myself

All over in a fine oil

The Book of SOL

My velvet robe my compliments

Hershey's dark chocolate skin

I begin to heat up while the wine chills

On the rocks the I roll out the

Soft sheets to my bed

Candles lit

Fragrances filling the air

Where do we start?

I do not care ...

But ....

I'm alone.

The Book of SOL

Anyone care for a little ...

One on one?

The Book of SOL

ME

Relating to others through words

Overworking myself at times

With God on my side

Don't doubt what I can do however

You would be surprised...

Some say I am greater than I know

Others are waiting on my fall

Love courses through my veins even for them

Obviously it's not easy to love enemies

The Book of SOL

More and more I humble myself daily

Over time because of this I elevate higher

Never will I truly know my limits because they are endless...

The Book of SOL

I LOOK AROUND

I look around and see much business for coroners

While we kill ourselves slowly drinking spirits on street corners

I look around and see abandoned houses on avenues

Where people live rent free bringing down the property's value

The Book of SOL

I look around and hear people speaking my

zingers

Hooked on everything else when cornichons

hooked on phonics

I look around and see most of women's

bodies

Because not wearing clothes or having them

too tight has become a hobby

I look around and see the acronyms the

norm

The Book of SOL

Because we are too lazy to spell now and

use words in the proper form

I look around and see men acting like boys

Toying with women so women would rather

play with toys

I look around and see babies having babies

And even then they have multiple partners

so daddy is a maybe

The Book of SOL

I look around and see men with pants too big or small

Still riding in packs yelling at women from across the mall

I look around and see us going in insane

Clubbing every weekend with the same hangover for days

I look around and see much procrastination

We talk about being real when we are the ones faking

The Book of SOL

I look around and see the lazy generation

Literally ignoring our forefathers demonstration

Of trying to come together and ignore the indignation

And form relationships instead of just 5 minute relations

So we can raise our babies and give them confirmation

That they can make it in this world and build a better nation

The Book of SOL

But frustration sets in along with bitter hatred

And we turn our backs on and start assassinating

Each other ....

No one to hear ....

No one to listen ...

No one to grab my hand and finish this ongoing mission

So I stand ...

The Book of SOL

And until we all see

I yell for unity! And while I wait for us to come together ...

I look around

The Book of SOL

FINALLY SOBER

I had a drink on the rocks, symbolizing that I had hit the bottom. I guess it was true.... She did have to be intoxicated to show me raw emotion to me... Spiritually or otherwise... which made me realize... I had been drunk for years. But now that I am sober and reality has hit... my head and shoulders hang over. I wish I could wash my memory away from the good times and the bad from then til now...

I remember my first time opening to her. It was like popping the cork on a wine bottle. I had been shaken over the years, so I poured out instantly with a little spillage. She

The Book of SOL

caught every drop of me as I poured out to her. Being as I was in a liquid state, I conformed to exactly what she wanted and evaporated into her sky.

I was in the clouds, looking down on what used to be my problems before I met her. Now, I was floating above them, with no care in the world. I was high in a euphoria... a crazy but mellow emotional individual that could only be handled by her. I guess that's why I was always so hot around her. She made my blood boil by the liter then cool to put me to sleep. What a sensation.

The Book of SOL

But now... that I have awakened. Now... that I am facing the world for what it really is and I have precipitated from the clouds. Now... that I have finally hit some surface from that abyss I was falling in. Though scattered... I stand... dazed but stable. One day soon, I will lift my head and embrace the sun beating down on it and show my face again. But for now, just know that.... I'm sober again.

The Book of SOL

VOID APOLOGY

I am sorry for what took place

But I do not apologize for loving you

Enough to be real in such

A fantasy world you live in

Through your days you act as if everything

Is perfect though your flaws show

When the sun hits

I respect you too much to spread your flaws

So I blanket them in a special place in my heart

Along with the rest of things you have done to me

The Book of SOL

I see you have moved on after out spat

Because I couldn't spit out how I felt

And for a while I hauled that burden around

Until its lease was up in my head

You said you made an attempt

And it's my turn

Well, I'm turning the other way

I will always love you

But it is clear I am the only one loving

Or even desiring to be in love

So I'm out

Of options, time and patience

I'm nothing to your anymore anyway

The Book of SOL

So even if I did see you in person to say it

It would be a void apology

So I will leave the situation and you

alone. Love always

The Book of SOL

PHOTO-SYNTHESIS

She's "rooted" within me. When hard times arise in our lives, she deepens into my soul Hard winds blow to and fro, but I am able to stand strong because of her. She provides for me like no other in order for me to survive. Yes, without her, I am nothing. She is the reason I "grow". When rain falls, she shelters me. She never "leaves" me.

I will never find another like her. There are many that look like her, but are all simply copies "scattered" all over. I could easily "pick" her out of a bouquet, a bushel or a patch, for she shines a special shine above all of the rest. When the sun hits her, her

The Book of SOL

features are magnified as she "blossoms" with beauty. Excuse me. I began to get excited thinking about it. Let me "settle". Mmmmmm. What a blessing....

Her "natural essence" is intoxicating. Her "soil" is rich and I know I have sown into good, "fertile ground." I reap a great "harvest" from doing so. I have learned that her thorns are not a defense mechanism, but they are instructions for me to know how to hold her just right. She is always open and always loving.

She is the light of my life and the apple of my eye. She is motivation for me daily to keep a smile, for I am a representation of her.

The Book of SOL

People see me and see her. People see her and see me. For we were "planted" the same as "seedlings" but "sprouted" as different genders. However, the winds "slipped" up and landed us in the same grass.

Nevertheless we are one mind, body and spirit occupying two different organisms, and that is why we have daily experiences of "photo-synthesis."

The Book of SOL

WITHDRAWAL

I guess I have to wean myself off of you... I tried the "cold turkey" approach, but you are much more addicting than I thought. Nicotine fits have nothing on the way I act without you. Every time I inhale your essence, I go higher and higher. You injected me with your poison through my ears, giving me an escape from all of my troubles. After this, I could always lay the "pipe." Everything becomes euphoric suddenly. You often unzipped my "fly" and "trapped" me in your world. You gave me a rush, which was why I was always in a rush to see you. Now I cannot for many reasons;

The Book of SOL

some are more serious than others. for the sake of your significant other and more personally, for my own well-being and health. I can't take the junk man's "itch" any longer, so there is no need to give me something to "scratch."

My mind cannot take any more of the "by any means necessary" concept. As I was doing some of the things I did to have I couldn't believe it was happening. It was a majesty of transactions between you and I with our actions but I began to feel like I was going through pseudo abstinence. Yes, your dose to me was constant for a while, but then you pulled back from me. I couldn't

The Book of SOL

tell you no because you were the dealer. Now I wander... Trying to keep my head up but I can't help but hang my head over the toilet due to my weak stomach...

I know I will get through this. It'll just take time. Yes, tis hard at the moment to even lie still, but I wonder if it is the same for you knowing that the man that lies next to you lies still... I guess I'd better worry about what I have on my plate and my plate only. I vowed that when I get back on my feet, this will never happen again. I will see to it that happens. However, pray for me in the meantime. Rehabilitation is a process to the mind, body and soul when you are going

The Book of SOL

through withdrawal... Hmph, ask Ray Charles.

NATURAL BEAUTY

Your face is an enchanting projection. It is a reward after each day from all of my stressors and straining. I love the security of your arms and the way your heart relaxes me as it beats the drum of my ear while I lay your breast. Your essence tickles and tempts my nose like a home cooked meal triggering a desire to an empty stomach. I am hungry for you... Your lips are a pool in which my tongue can dive in and go for a nice swim. I love the hazelnut tone you have, complementing the other butter pecan and chocolate parts of you that are often covered

The Book of SOL

until you see fit to bless one's eyes with such a scene.

Do not feel compelled to cover any part of you that you feel is imperfect. I am in awe of those features. Trust that you do not have more "love" than I can "handle." Trust that you don't have to "stretch" your clothes to cover any "marks." Let me see you for who you really are. Don't "makeup" something about yourself to impress me. Let me kiss the "lines" on your forehead. Let's not stick to a traditional "script." Show me your hair. You don't need assistance, seeing as I don't care about good or nappy roots. I won't be

The Book of SOL

the type of guy to "split" when we can't make "ends" meet.

I don't wish to lay on "plastic" that you received from "surgery." God gave you a perfect amount of everything so I don't need to see "scars" from "reduction." My love is big enough to wrap around you three times regardless of size. Let's shape our future. Let's see eye to eye. Quit hiding them behind a "shadow." Our connection and faith is enough "foundation" for us to go on. Let the cool breeze hit your neck and chin raising the "whiskers" you have to symbolize the feisty feline you are. I love all

The Book of SOL

of you... Your... everything. So show me...

your natural beauty.

The Book of SOL

REPLACING THE REPLACEMENT

Make up with no break up

But you are still attached to the person

So with each new person you meet

Your condition worsens

Trying to forget that person

But just can't let go

So you become easily influenced

So whatever they ask you say "Let's go"

Never taking time to heal your broken heart

Never taking time to get a fresh new start

Never rebuilding, just hiding the debris

The Book of SOL

Only appearing to be happy and smiling with glee

Sexting, flirting, kissing trying to feel a void

Multiple sex partners and you are still annoyed

Because you're still holding onto the one original

They have your everything... physical, mental, spiritual...

Take time out for you learn about yourself

Quit searching for solace in bottles clubs and everyone else

Learn to love yourself and have a recovery time

The Book of SOL

Let go of past endeavors... the mind was not designed

To hold such nonsense, hear me please, fully move on

Or if you feel they are the one follow your heart... go home

That can happen too... don't have me mistaken

But it's not healthy to have one after the other

With no time in between....

You're only replacing replacements

Find that one... then the others won't matter

GAY

Pain...

My friend, my enemy

Scarred bruised

Battered used

Humiliated skewed

By women for all types of use

I'm through...

I give up on love

And give in to reality

Naturally I'm a fallacy

That is not good I'm balancing

With the opposite

The Book of SOL

I'm supposed to be attracted to

Since my worth is dirt cheap

They hurt me

Burn me shock me

But no longer surprise me

Lying, cheating

Secret meetings

Hidden texts

And deleted messages

Not to mention neglect

Are child's play to me now

Pictures flirting

With people they feel worthy

The Book of SOL

Leading them to the room

While leading me on

Has left me off

So I turn to the only way I

Know to go...

I had "1" last nerve

And it has been turned "80" degrees

I have done all I can

Maybe I'll do better with a man

I have nothing else to say

I'm gay

The Book of SOL

SEE ABOUT ME

Awakening every day from the

Noise of a small heater or fan

Working a job for hours

Feeling like I am paid for minutes

At wit's end worrying about how

I am going to make ends meet...

Trying not to break the law

To pay my bills

The Book of SOL

Saying farewell to items I

Have to pawn

So the rent man can pass me by/bye

Puzzled on how I ended up here

Picking the pieces up of a

Broken heart from being used

And humiliated by so many

So many times it became a norm

Begging for a way out

The Book of SOL

Being choked by stress

Stipulated by circumstances

Pinned down by problems

Looking around for help

And no one is there...

Left and right... all I see

Is walls closing in

Everyone has left

Even though I did them right

The Book of SOL

Mine enemies seem blessed

With no worries or troubles

Love knows me no more

Success is foreign

Hope was lost somewhere

Along the way with my mind

Faith is dwindling like

The foundation of a

Dry-rotted apartment

The Book of SOL

I can't see my way

Lord...

Please...

Come see about me

SUCCESSFUL

Born with a darker shade

Categorized by a race not

Won by the swift

Known by nine numbers

Like a toy on an assembly line

Just another statistic...

Expected to do something that will

Ultimately make him amount to nothing

The Book of SOL

Making the last chapter of his life

The longest chapter becoming a rapper

Behind bars

A hero to the streets,

A villain to the community...

Said to contribute to a seed or two

To be conceived and

After-words with the baby's mother

He is considered a dead beat

And may wind up dead or beaten

The Book of SOL

Scared or swindled

By an unfair system in which

He will never win...

In old age if he makes it

Trying to be "social"

With little "security" of funds

Due to disability

Telling stories to people that

Aren't entirely true

Spreading wisdom living

The Book of SOL

In past events

Singing should haves and

Could haves

My father... my grandfather...

This won't be me I declare

I refuse to be what the world

Thinks I am

I will be one way or another

Successful

ONE MORE TIME

We see each other in a distance every day

Only laws and time keep us apart

Your voice and smell carry on the wind

I hear you… I smell you

You keep me alive as you drive by

My heart skips a beat for that glance

And that connection with no words

Just a smile or a sense

Does that make sense?

Maybe but not most

They don't understand what we have

What we had…

The Book of SOL

But I will wait baby

I know we had a misunderstanding

But our battle is almost over

On both ends

Soon the only candles we will

Burn is our own at dinner

I'll be here sweetheart

Even if in life I only see you

One more time

The Book of SOL

NEVER STOPPED LOVING YOU

When I was six you went missing

I heard some loud shouts and a door slam

Little did I know you had walked out

Or a least... that's what was told to me

Mom said she's still waiting on the bread

But I realized I couldn't live on that alone

So I decided to hustle to survive

With fast lane living ignoring signs

Because it felt good to provide

The humility of puberty

The mystery of facial hair

The Book of SOL

The tornado of mood swings

All of which I needed you

But couldn't be with you

But now I have grown into

A grown man

And I am doing the best I can

For mine...

So I can say man to man

I understand dad

I forgive you...

And I never stopped loving you

The Book of SOL

HOLDING ON

The cliffs of life have me
Hanging on by a "thread" sometimes
Sometimes I can't pull up
It would be easier to get a camel
Through the eye of a "needle"
Sometimes I feel like breaking
The "law" to pay my "bills"
Sometimes I feel like
Giving "up" because burdens have
Me so weighed "down"
Talk about a roller coaster of emotions
But I have learned to find a hint of joy
In the clues we miss and take
For granted while we wait for a blessing
To be granted from above
A hug... A smile... A soothing voice or
An encouraging word from a pure heart
And thick and thin friend
A nice meal every now and then
Doesn't hurt either
The real valuables...

The Book of SOL

That don't cost a thing but time
We are not willing to spend because
We are too busy spending money
And trying to find the right ingredients
To make more...
So distasteful...
Though most times I am broke
To the naked eye
I am richer than my wildest dreams
Because of what my grandma taught me...
Thank you grandma
Despite a circumstance
I will never sit down on what I know
God has me
And I know to always do what you taught me
I will keep holding on

The Book of SOL

LET MY WORD'S WORKS SPEAK FOR ME

(THE POET'S PRAYER)

This poem is based on the bible scripture John 10:38.

Dear Lord, I kneel to you now with a bowed head and a humble pen. I first must give thanks to you for my ability to lay pen to paper, for it is you who gives these divine words power. Yea, you have given me a mighty task to create lyrical miracles, but you have also assigned me my own styles and genres. I pray for an open heart with patience and discernment covering

The Book of SOL

every letter that passes through. Do not allow me to be anxious for any posting of my work for people to perceive and marvel my pieces. I ask for a steady hand to paint pictures never seen before in dialogue. I ask for a sound mind to withstand any negativity that may try to nullify my notions. Let the wisdom that I write be worn on the backs of t-shirts and hung in bathrooms and jazz clubs. Let my creativity be discussed over cups of coffee and book reviews. Contrarily, do not allow me to become boastful in my own diction making popularity an addiction...

The Book of SOL

Grant me the gift of giving you glory in my stanzas. Shine light on my pen and direct me to where you wish my writing should go. Let the ink flow as the precious fountain that is free to all as a healing stream up at Calvary's Mountain. Let ruptured souls find peace in my rhythms. Alas, do not let me sway from the path you have set for me deterring others from their paths just the same as they read my work. Let me yield not to temptation to use my gift for evil, but rather deliver others from it. Let the tears I shed on the page be evaporated and rain down showers of blessings to readers. Give my hand the unremitting strength to never let go of my pen and write in and out of

The Book of SOL

season. Let me put my life in my words, laying down my life on paper as your Son laid down his for me.

Father... O Father... Give me the confidence and tolerance of a slave. Motivate my mind to never back down and always drive forward. As the blood drips from my fingers from holding on oh so tight... Let me drive forward. As the rain hits my pages let me guard them with my life... Let me drive forward. As people try to twist the meaning of my sayings, humble me in professionalism and find favor upon me. Let me drive forward. When arthritis sets in and I can barely lift my hands... Let

The Book of SOL

me drive forward. When this body finally fails me and breath has left this body O'Lord... When my hands can do no more and my brain is finally thought free. When my soul has ascended, though many told me to go to hell for simply speaking the truth. I do not ask for pity. I do not ask for a memorial. I do not request for my name to be remembered in lights forever. Father, all I desire... all I am working for... Is to essentially without a shadow of a doubt... leave my life on paper. If they change not but one life, that is enough for me, because my work was not in vain... Let my word's works speak for me.

The Book of SOL

Author Rowdy Solomon Jr.

Aka

SOL

Books by R. D. Solomon Jr.

A LOVE WAR: TWISTED

www.ingramcontent.com/pod-product-compliance
Lightning Source LLC
Chambersburg PA
CBHW031407040426
42444CB00005B/459